G LF
QUOTES

ISBN : 0-931089-02-6   Printed in Hong Kong

Dedicated to those who believe that golf is like a love affair... If you don't take it too seriously, it's no fun, and if you do take it seriously it breaks your heart.

"I don't say my golf game is bad; but if I grew tomatoes, they'd come up sliced."

Miller Barber
Professional golfer

"I'd give up golf
    if I didn't have so
    many sweaters."

Bob Hope
Comedian

G3

"Water holes are sacrificial waters where you make a steady gift of your pride and high-priced balls."

Tommy Bolt
Professional golfer

"My best score ever is 103, but I've only been playing 15 years."

Alex Karras
Detroit Lions defensive lineman

"For most amateurs, the best wood in the bag is the pencil."

Chi Chi Rodriguez
Professional golfer

G7

"There are two things not long for this world - dogs that chase cars and golfers who chip for pars."

Lee Trevino
Professional Golfer

"Give me golf clubs,
   fresh air and a beautiful
   partner, and you can
   keep my golf clubs and
   the fresh air."

Jack Benny
Comedian

"The only reason I played golf was so I could afford to go hunting or fishing."

Sam Snead
Professional Golfer

"Competitive golf is played mainly on a five-and-a-half-inch course, the space between your ears."

Bobby Jones
Amateur golfer

"Golf is a good
walk spoiled."

Mark Twain
Writer

G13

"The only shots you can be dead sure of are those you've had already."

Byron Nelson
Professional golfer

"I shot a wild elephant in Africa 30 yards from me, and it didn't hit the ground until it was right at my feet. I wasn't a bit scared. But a 4 foot putt scares me to death."

Sam Snead
Professional golfer

"When I'm on a course and it starts to rain and lightning, I hold up my one iron, 'cause I know even God can't hit a one iron."

Lee Trevino
Professional golfer

"Being a left-handed golfer is a big advantage. No one knows enough about your swing to mess you up with advice."

Bob Charles
Professional golfer

"Hey, is this room out of bounds?"

Alex Karras
Detroit Lions defensive lineman, to a startled employee, after hitting a golf ball off the first tee through a large plate glass window in the clubhouse

G19

"Through years of experience I have found that air offers less resistance than dirt."

Jack Nicklaus
Professional golfer, when asked why he tees up his ball so high

"You start to choke when you drive through the front gate. On the first hole, you just want to make contact with the ball."

Hale Irwin
Professional golfer, on the Masters

''What other people may find in poetry or art museums, I find in the flight of a good drive - the white ball sailing up into the blue sky, growing smaller and smaller, then suddenly reaching its apex, curving, falling and finally dropping to the turf to roll some more, just the way I planned it.''

Arnold Palmer
Professional golfer

"The sport isn't like any other where a player can take out all that is eating him on an opponent. In golf, it's strictly you against your clubs."

Bob Rosburg
Professional golfer

"Selecting a stroke is like selecting a wife. To each his own."

Ben Hogan
Professional golfer, on putting

"Golf is the only sport I know of where a player pays for every mistake. A man can muff a serve in tennis, miss a strike in baseball, or throw an incomplete pass in football, and still have another chance to square himself. But in golf, every swing counts against you."

Lloyd Mangrum
Professional golfer

"I'm hitting the woods just great, but I'm having a terrible time getting out of them."

Harry Toscano
Professional golfer

G27

"I think most of the rules of golf stink. They were written by the guys who can't even break a hundred."

Chi Chi Rodriguez
Professional golfer

"Golf is a compromise between what your ego wants you to do, what experience tells you to do, and what your nerves let you do."

Bruce Crampton
Professional golfer

"Golf is not a game of great shots. It's a game of the most accurate misses. The people who win make the smallest mistakes."

Gene Littler
Professional golfer

"The older I get,
... the better I
use to be."

Lee Trevino
Professional golfer

"I can airmail the golf ball, but sometimes I don't put the right address on it."

Jim Dent
Professional golfer known for his long tee shots

"The mind messes up more shots than the body."

Tommy Bolt
Professional golfer

"Anything I want it to be. For instance, this hole right here is a par 47 - and yesterday I birdied the sucker."

Willie Nelson
Singer, when asked what par is on a golf course he purchased near Austin, Texas

The first one is called "How to Get the Most Distance Out of Your Shanks," and the other is, "How to Take the Correct Stance On Your Fourth Putt."

Lee Trevino
Professional golfer, on his new books

"I play in the low 80's. If it's any hotter than that, I won't play."

Joe E. Louis
Comedian

G37

"It is nothing new or original to say that golf is played one stroke at a time. But it took me many strokes to realize it."

Bobby Jones
Amateur golfer

"You drive for show and putt for dough."

Al Balding
Professional golfer

"You don't hit anything with your backswing. So don't rush it."

Doug Ford
Professional golfer

"Golf is a way of testing ourselves while enjoying ourselves."

Arnold Palmer
Professional golfer

"Golf is 90 percent inspiration and 10 percent perspiration."

Johnny Miller
Professional golfer

"It matters not the sacrifice
which makes the duffer's
wife so sore.
I am the captive of my
slice.
I am the servant of my
score."

Grantland Rice
Sportswriter

"There are no points for style when it comes to putting. It's getting the ball to drop that counts."

Brian Swarbrick
Professional golfer

"You can talk to a fade, but a hook won't listen."

Lee Trevino
Professional golfer

"If there is any larceny in a man, golf will bring it out."

Paul Gallico
Sportswriter

G47

''Golf is like a razor. You get just so sharp and then it begins to dull a little the more you use it.''

Doug Sanders
Professional golfer on overpracticing

"Serenity is knowing that your worst shot is still going to be pretty good."

Johnny Miller
Professional golfer

"If you watch a game, it's fun. If you play it, it's recreation. If you work at it, it's golf."

Bob Hope
Comedian

"Golf— A young man's vice and an old man's penance."

Irvin Cobb
Humorist

"There is absolutely nothing humorous at the Masters. Here, small dogs do not bark and babies do not cry."

Gary Player
Professional golfer

"It's always hard to sleep when you've got a big early lead. You just lay there and smile at the ceiling all night."

Dave Stockton
Professional golfer

"If you are going to throw a club, it is important to throw it ahead of you, down the fairway, so you don't waste energy going back to pick it up."

Tommy Bolt
Professional golfer

G54

"If you have to remind yourself to concentrate during competition, you've got no chance to concentrate."

Bobby Nichols
Professional golfer

"In every tournament there are a few rounds of super golf; without a doubt they are played subconsciously."

Chick Evans, Jr.
Amateur golfer

"You can be the greatest iron player in the world or the greatest putter, but if you can't get the ball in position to use your greatness, you can't win."

Ben Hogan
Professional golfer, on the importance of drives

"When God wants to play through, you let him play through."

Lee Trevino
Professional golfer, after being struck by lightning

G59

"Golf— A game in which one endeavors to control a ball with implements ill adapted for the purpose."

Woodrow Wilson
Twenty-eighth President of the United States, defining the sport

"If a lot of people gripped a knife and fork like they do a golf club, they'd starve to death."

Sam Snead
Professional golfer

"If you want to beat somebody on the golf course, just get him mad."

Dave Williams
Professional golfer

"When the squirrels and birds see us on the tee, they start scattering. We've set back the mating season in Texas 90 days."

John Plumbley
Rice golf coach, on his team's driving

"Golf is the only game where the worst player gets the best of it. They obtain more out of it with regard to both exercise and enjoyment. The good player gets worried over the slightest mistake, whereas the poor player makes too many mistakes to worry over them."

David Lloyd George

"Golf is an ideal diversion, but a ruinous disease."

Bertie Charles Forbes
Magazine editor

"Eighteen holes of match
  play will teach
  you more about your foe
  than 19 years of dealing
  with him across a
  desk."

Grantland Rice
Sportswriter

"In golf, driving is a game of free swinging muscle control, while putting is something like performing eye surgery and using a bread knife for the scalpel."

Tommy Bolt
Professional golfer

"One of the old pro's, when asked why he hardly ever took a practice swing before hitting his drives and long approaches, is reported to have said: ''I don't want to waste it 'cause it might be the good one.''

"The average expert player - if he's lucky - hits 6, 8, or 10 real good shots in a round. The rest are real good misses."

Tommy Armour
Professional golfer

"Any game where a man 60 can beat a man 30 ain't no game."

Burt Shotten
Major league baseball manager

"Golf: A game where the ball always lies poorly and players well."

"Golf is a game where guts, stick-to-itiveness and blind devotion will always net you absolutely nothing but an ulcer."

Tommy Bolt
Professional golfer

"In golf as in life it's the follow through that makes the difference."

"Golf: The worst damn fun anybody ever had."

Cy Manier
Professional golfer

G75

Other Golf Gifts Products:

- *The Complete Golfer's Handbook*
- *100 Sure Ways to Sharpen Your Game*
- *Golf Quotes*
- *The Ladies Tee*
- *Games Golfers Play*
- Scoring Log
- *Golf Tips*
- Golf Diary
- Links to the Past
- Ball Marker Collector
- Tee-Cup
- Pocket Pointers®
- *Birdies in the Oven*

- *Aces in the Kitchen*
- Behold the Golfer
- Party-Pak
- Golf Napkins
- Collectible Prints
- Brass Golf Plaques
- Golf Notes
- Towel Caddie
- T-Marks
- "In the Rough" Greeting Cards
- Holiday Cards
- *The Trouble with Tennis*
- *Fishing Lines*

GOLF GIFTS INC.
219 Eisenhower Lane South • Lombard, IL 60148
1-800-552-4430 • (708) 953-9087